essence of WHITE

Hilary Mandleberg

essence of WHITE

RYLAND
PETERS
& SMALL

Designer   Luis Peral-Aranda
Location Research   Nadine Bazar and Kate Brunt
Production   Patricia Harrington
Head of Design   Gabriella Le Grazie
Publishing Director   Anne Ryland

First published in the United Kingdom in 2000
by Ryland Peters & Small
Cavendish House, 51–55 Mortimer Street,
London W1N 7TD
10 9 8 7 6 5 4 3 2 1

Printed and bound in China by Toppan
Printing Co.

ISBN 1 84172 032 1

A CIP record for this book is available from
the British Library.

contents

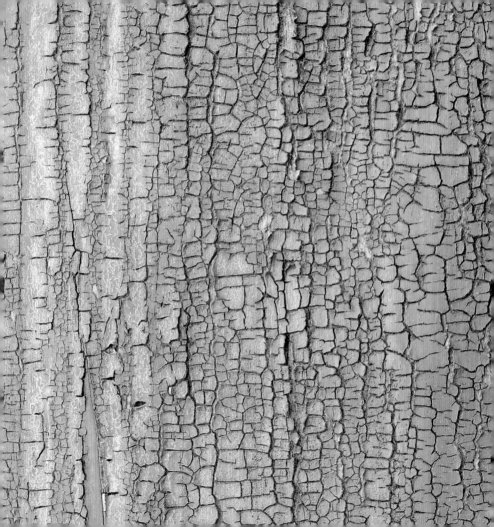

shades & textures

If all the earth were paper white

John Lyly

Nature so rarely manages to achieve pure white. Freshly fallen snow with sunlight bouncing off it or white clouds scudding across a clear blue sky may come close, but just see how a small hollow in the snow casts a shadow of blue or how the thinned-out

SHADES OF WHITE

edges of the clouds are a wistful pale grey. And if you thought that a white flower was white, then look again. Bright yellow stamens pour out a rich buttermilk pool. Petals are coloured shyly with a soft blush or glow gently green in the reflection of the leaves.

White is gently romantic or starkly modern, depending on how you use it. With sunlight filtering through, even

a heavy canvas curtain can look light and airy, while a classic metal lamp sheds a cool and otherworldly glow.

Does white conjure up an image of clinical cleanliness, stark utility or just the boringly bland? It need not. Texture is the secret ingredient that brings white to life and turns it into an exciting sensory experience. The subtle interplay of light and shade as

TEXTURES

light reflects off a surface lets you distinguish between gauzy fine white muslin, the delicately fragile petals of a simple white flower, sparkling white enamelled cooking pans, crunchy lace, freshly starched damask, or the flat matt density of white-painted walls.

Mix your textures to liven up white-on-white decorating schemes. Stick to natural materials, irregular surfaces

and organic elements for a country feel, or smoothly finished man-made details for a more contemporary look.

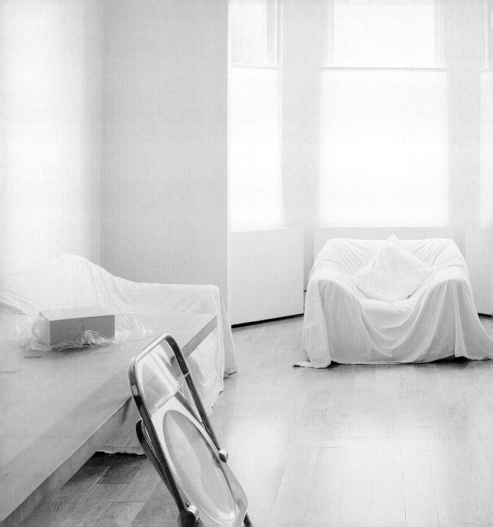

living/dining

What could be more soothing than a living room painted in the purest of whites? An all-white backdrop will emphasize the shape and texture of objects in the room – an antique wooden bowl, a battered painted table or a shiny leather chair. And as the day

CLASSIC WHITE

progresses and the light moves around the room, white shows itself to be infinitely complex, a far cry from monochrome. These are the subtleties that help to make it a classic. But ever since decorating first began, achieving the perfect white has been

something of an obsession. People
have tried anything and everything -
crushed and powdered bones, pearls,

shells - but the results were dirty off-
whites or whites that quickly turned
yellow. Then, in the 1920s, titanium

white was born. This wonder pigment is permanent, non-toxic, does not go yellow and covers well. Soon it was

adopted by the modernists as their signature colour. Now we wonder how we ever managed without pure white.

White is the classic colour choice for elegant dining. It creates the relaxed mood you need for good digestion and shows food off to its best advantage.

DINING IN WHITE

kitchen

Working in a serene, uncluttered white kitchen will help any cook stay calm in a crisis. To create the effect of an airy sun-drenched beach house kitchen, choose white walls, stripped floorboards, pale wood counter tops and matching dining table. A solitary

NOW AND ZEN

dark wood armoire, a trio of woven baskets and a simple carved wooden bowl, together with a white orchid in a dark ceramic pot, will add just a hint of subtly restrained contrast and understated eastern elegance and will add to the deep sense of tranquility.

Gleaming white surfaces positively shriek 'germ-free', which makes white the ideal choice for the ultimate hygienic kitchen. If your taste veers towards the monastic, then you'll love the sharp, uncluttered lines of flush white doors, stainless steel and clean-cut marble. Everything in its place and a place for everything. Introduce a slightly softer but no less business-like note with wooden counter tops and the occasional wooden cupboard front or add cosiness to an all-white kitchen with a thoughtfully chosen display of utensils that bridges the gap between modern and country. And if it's nostalgia you're after, try a splashback of bevel-edged white tiles.

bedroom

All that we see or seem
Is but a dream within a dream

Edgar Allan Poe

Floaty, filmy, feminine and fantastic! Deck out a bedroom in romantic white for a voluptuous, sensual experience. Fairy-tale beds in warmly gleaming mahogany or sinuous cast iron entice you to your nightly slumber. Pure white antique cotton sheets and soft,

DREAMING IN WHITE

down-filled pillows embrace you while you dream. Recreate a vanished world of romance and elegance with gauzy billowing drapes and cupboards that open to reveal a neat stack of crisply ironed and folded bed linen. This is the ~~stuff that dreams are made~~ of.

Meditate on white to lift your spirits, for white is the colour of peace and comfort, the colour that alleviates sadness, cleanses the emotions and works to purify the soul. Used in the bedroom, white is gently soothing and conducive to sleep. Pared-down, fuss-free white for walls and bedding is perfection for the ultimate, minimal bedroom. But take care, for white can also be cold and isolating. Add the warmth of wood or a blend of shades and textures, then feel the serenity.

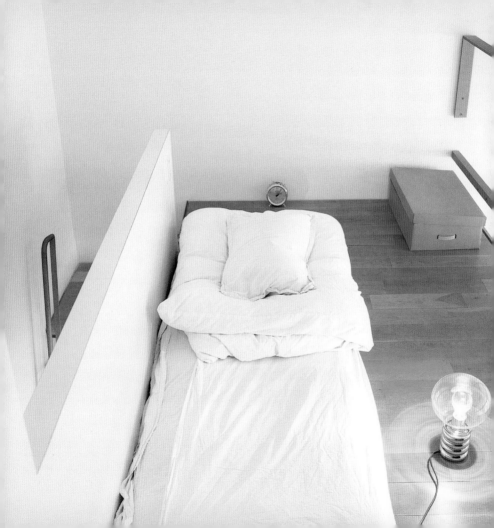

Lightness and a sense of space go hand in hand with white, and this cool, slightly oriental bedroom shows why.

Subtle light effects, minimal furniture and an expanse of window with just a hint of a blind accentuate the mood.

bathroom

Baths and showers are often tucked away in the smallest, gloomiest room in the house. What better way to make them feel spacious than to create an all-white bathroom around them? For long bath-time soaks, imagine sinking deep into a huge old-fashioned white-

BATHING BELLE

enamelled bath with claw feet, then wrapping up in a soft white bathrobe. For quick getaways, modern minimal white is the no-nonsense choice. And so minimal doesn't end up as clinical, add some natural texture – touches of wood, pumice, cork and real sponge.

. . . a white celestial thought

Henry Vaughan

White is famous as a symbol of purity and cleanliness which is why it came to be associated with sanitation. Once,

sanitary fittings only came in white. All that has long since changed, but white remains a bathroom favourite.

outside

White makes a glorious choice for gardens. Scintillatingly bright in the sun, it looks great in shady corners too. Enjoy the luminous contrast of white flowers against dark foliage, particularly on summer evenings, and remember that, since white recedes,

SUN OR SHADE

white blooms at the end of the garden will make it appear longer. Clothe a garden in scented white jasmine for the ultimate night-time sensory experience or bring the Mediterranean look to even the smallest of courtyards by painting it white, right down to its flowerpots.

A cluster of limewashed
houses dazzles the eye
in the summer sun. For
many centuries, especially
in hot climates, limewash
has been used to help
keep bricks and plaster,
stables and outhouses
cool and clean. It bonds
with the surface to form
a thin layer of lime that
acts as a disinfectant.
In many parts of the
world, the annual visit
from the itinerant lime-
washer is still one of
the highlights of the
spring-cleaning season.

White furniture can blend effortlessly with any garden setting, traditional or contemporary. And it's so easy to

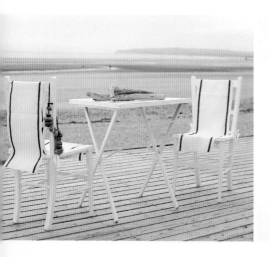

dress up inexpensive junk-shop finds to make original, funky pieces. Just rub down wood or metal, then apply one or two coats of white paint. If you're feeling adventurous, transform a white cotton roller towel and a few

pieces of tape into a seat cover, or beautify a tired old director's chair with a loose cover made from canvas.

credits

Architects and designers whose work is featured in this book;

Key: **a**=above, **b**=below, **l**=left, **r**=right, **t**=telephone, **f**=fax

Barefoot Elegance

Dot Spikings & Jennifer Castle

Interior Designers

3537 Old Coneyo Road

Suite 105

Newbury Park

CA91320

USA

t 00 1 805 499 5959

Pages 20, 30

Alexandra Champalimaud & Associates Inc.

Interior Architecture and Design

One Union Square West

Suite 603

New York

NY 10003

USA

t 00 1 212 807 8869

f 00 1 212 807 1742

Page 52

Françoise Dorget

Interior Designer

Caravane

6 rue Pavée

75004 Paris

France

t 00 33 (0)1 44 61 04 20

f 00 33 (0)1 44 61 04 22

Pages 56, 58-59

Mark Guard Architects

161 Whitfield Street

London W1P 5RY

t 00 44 (0)20 7380 1199

Pages 44-45

Alastair Hendy

Food writer, art director and designer

f 00 44 (0)20 7739 6040

Page 29 **l** & **r**

Littman Goddard Hogarth

Architects

12 Chelsea Wharf

15 Lots Road

London

SW10 0QJ

t 00 44 (0)20 7351 7871

Pages 2, 22 **r**

Roger Oates Design

Specialist in English flatweave rugs and runners

The Long Barn

Eastnor

Ledbury

Herefordshire

HR8 1EL

t 00 44 (0)1531 632718

Pages 19 **r**, 24-25

Vicente Wolf Associates Inc.

Architects

333 West 39th Street

New York

NY 10018

USA

t 00 1 212 465 0590

Page 23 **l**

Woolf Architects

39-51 Highgate Road

London NW5 1RT

t 00 44 (0)20 7428 9500

Pages 4-5, 18, 33 main & inset **b**, 34 **al**, 43

photographers